HomeBuilders Cou

MW01062544

overcoming Stress
in Your Marriage

By Doug Daily

FAMILYLIFE™
Bringing Timeless Principles Home
Little Rock, Arkansas

Loveland, Colorado

Group's R.E.A.L. Guarantee® to you:

This Group resource incorporates our R.E.A.L. approach to ministry—one that encourages long-term retention and life transformation. It's ministry that's:

Relational
Because learner-to-learner interaction enhances learning and builds Christian friendships.

Experiential
Because what learners experience through discussion and action sticks with them up to 9 times longer than what they simply hear or read.

Applicable
Because the aim of Christian education is to equip learners to be both hearers and doers of God's Word.

Learner-based
Because learners understand and retain more when the learning process takes into consideration how they learn best.

Overcoming Stress in Your Marriage

Copyright © 2001 Doug Daily

Visit our Web site: **www.grouppublishing.com**

Credits
FamilyLife
Editor: David Boehi

Group Publishing, Inc.
Editor: Matt Lockhart
Creative Development Editor: Paul Woods
Chief Creative Officer: Joani Schultz
Copy Editor: Lyndsay E. Bierce
Art Directors: Jenette L. McEntire and Helen Harrison
Cover Art Director: Jeff A. Storm
Computer Graphic Artist: Stephen Beer
Cover Photographer: Daniel Treat
Illustrator: Ken Jacobsen
Production Manager: Peggy Naylor

Unless otherwise noted, Scripture taken from the HOLY BIBLE, NEW INTERNA-TIONAL VERSION®. Copyright © 1973, 1978, 1984 by International Bible Society. Used by permission of Zondervan Publishing House. All rights reserved.

ISBN 0-7644-2245-6
15 14 13 12 11 10 9 8   09 08 07 06 05 04

Printed in the United States of America.

How to Let the Lord Build Your House
and not labor in vain

●

The HomeBuilders Couples Series®: A small-group Bible study dedicated to making your family all that God intended.

FamilyLife is a division of Campus Crusade for Christ International, an evangelical Christian organization founded in 1951 by Bill Bright. FamilyLife was started in 1976 to help fulfill the Great Commission by strengthening marriages and families and then equipping them to go to the world with the gospel of Jesus Christ. The FamilyLife Marriage Conference is held in most major cities throughout the United States and is one of the fastest-growing marriage conferences in America today. "FamilyLife Today," a daily radio program hosted by Dennis Rainey, is heard on hundreds of stations across the country. Information on all resources offered by FamilyLife may be obtained by contacting us at the address, telephone number, or World Wide Web site listed below.

Dennis Rainey, Executive Director
FamilyLife
P.O. Box 8220
Little Rock, AR 72221-8220
1-800-FL-TODAY
www.familylife.com

A division of Campus Crusade for Christ International
Bill Bright, Founder
Steve Douglass, President

About the Sessions

Each session in this study is composed of the following categories: Warm-Up, Blueprints, Wrap-Up, and HomeBuilders Project. A description of each of these categories follows:

Warm-Up (15 minutes)

 The purpose of Warm-Up is to help people unwind from a busy day and get to know each other better. Typically the first point in Warm-Up is an exercise that is meant to be fun while introducing the topic of the session. The ability to share in fun with others is important in building relationships. Another component of Warm-Up is the Project Report (except in Session One), which is designed to provide accountability for the HomeBuilders Project that is to be completed by couples between sessions.

Blueprints (60 minutes)

This is the heart of the study. In this part of each session, people answer questions related to the topic of study and look to God's Word for understanding. Some of the questions are to be answered by couples, in subgroups, or in the group at large. There are notes in the margin or instructions within a question that designate these groupings.

Wrap-Up (15 minutes)

This category serves to "bring home the point" and wind down a session in an appropriate fashion.

HomeBuilders Project (60 minutes)

This project is the unique application step in a HomeBuilders study. Before leaving a meeting, couples are encouraged to "Make a Date" to do the project for the session prior to the next meeting. Most HomeBuilders Projects contain three sections: (1) As a Couple—a brief exercise designed to get the date started; (2) Individually—a section of questions for husbands and wives to answer separately; and (3) Interact as a Couple—an opportunity for couples to share their answers with each other and to make application in their lives.

In addition to the above regular features, occasional activities are labeled "For Extra Impact." These are activities that generally provide a more active or visual way to make a particular point. Be mindful that people within a group have different learning styles. While most of what is presented is verbal, a visual or active exercise now and then helps engage more of the senses and appeals to people who learn best by seeing, touching, and doing.

About the Author

Doug Daily is a teaching pastor at Grace Church in Little Rock, Arkansas. He is a graduate of Mississippi State University and Dallas Theological Seminary and also earned a doctorate in ministry from Bethel Seminary. Doug and his wife, Patty, speak at FamilyLife Marriage Conferences and live in Little Rock. They have three children.

Contents

Acknowledgments

I would like to thank my wife, Patty, and my children—Josh, Daniel, and Laura—for graciously granting me the time and giving me the encouragement to undertake one more project. I'm also indebted to Dave Boehi, whose insightful challenges to my thoughts did to this study what fire does to iron—refines it into something useful.

Introduction

When a man and woman are married, they stand before a room of witnesses and proclaim their commitment to a lifetime of love. They recite a sacred vow "to have and to hold...from this day forward...to love, honor, and cherish...for better, for worse...for richer, for poorer...in sickness and in health...as long as we both shall live."

It's a happy day, perhaps the happiest in their lives. And yet, once the honeymoon ends, once the emotions of courtship and engagement subside, many couples realize that "falling in love" and building a good marriage are two different things. Keeping those vows is much more difficult than they thought it would be.

Otherwise intelligent people, who would not think of buying a car, investing money, or even going to the grocery store without some initial planning, enter into marriage with no plan of how to make that relationship succeed.

But God has already provided the plan, a set of blueprints for building a truly God-honoring marriage. His plan is designed to enable a man and woman to grow together in a mutually satisfying relationship and then to reach out to others with the love of Christ. Ignoring this plan leads only to isolation and separation between husband and wife. It's a pattern evident in so many homes today: Failure to follow God's blueprints results in wasted effort, bitter disappointment, and, in far too many cases, divorce.

In response to this need in marriages today, FamilyLife has developed a series of small-group studies called the HomeBuilders Couples Series.

You could complete this study alone with your spouse, but we strongly urge you to either form or join a group of couples studying this material. You will find that the questions in each session not only help you grow closer to your spouse, but they help create a special environment of warmth and fellowship as you study together how to build the type of marriage you desire. Participating in a HomeBuilders group could be one of the highlights of your married life.

The Bible: Your Blueprints for a God-Honoring Marriage

You will notice as you proceed through this study that the Bible is used frequently as the final authority on issues of life and marriage. Although written thousands of years ago, this Book still speaks clearly and powerfully about the conflicts and struggles faced by men and women. The Bible is God's Word—his blueprints for building a God-honoring home and for dealing with the practical issues of living.

We encourage you to have a Bible with you for each session. For this series we use the New International Version as our primary reference. Another excellent translation is the New American Standard Bible.

Ground Rules

Each group session is designed to be enjoyable and informative—and nonthreatening. Three simple ground rules will help ensure that everyone feels comfortable and gets the most out of the experience:

1. Don't share anything that would embarrass your spouse.

2. You may pass on any question you don't want to answer.

3. If possible, plan to complete the HomeBuilders Project as a couple between group sessions.

A Few Quick Notes About Leading a HomeBuilders Group

1. Leading a group is much easier than you may think! A group leader in a HomeBuilders session is really a "facilitator." As a facilitator, your goal is simply to guide the group through the discussion questions. You don't need to teach the material—in fact, we don't want you to! The special dynamic of a HomeBuilders group is that couples teach themselves.

2. This material is designed to be used in a home study, but it also can be adapted for use in a Sunday school environment. (See page 103 for more information about this option.)

3. We have included a section of Leader's Notes in the back of this book. Be sure to read through these notes before leading a session; they will help you prepare.

4. For more material on leading a HomeBuilders group, get a copy of the *HomeBuilders Leader Guide*, by Drew and Kit Coons. This book is an excellent resource that provides helpful guidelines on how to start a study, how to keep discussion moving, and much more.

A Word About Stress

I find it ironic that soon after beginning to write a HomeBuilders study on stress in marriage, my world turned upside down! Over the years I've learned to live with the stress of a pastor's life, but this was something else.

It began a few days before Christmas with a statement that would make any parent weak-kneed: "Your son Daniel has another brain tumor." With those words God put us on a path we had been down before but did not want to travel again. Two years earlier Daniel had been diagnosed with a brain tumor. Doctors had ended up removing a tumor about the size of an egg, and he had not shown any aftereffects. But now, at age fourteen, another tumor had appeared.

To our great relief, Daniel's second surgery went well. But then a few days later, my mother-in-law went in for a routine physical, and doctors found a spot in her lung. A needle biopsy confirmed our fears. It was cancer. She had survived breast cancer twenty-six years earlier and colon cancer eight years ago. Now her lungs! Both Daniel and my mother-in-law would be in the hospital less than a mile apart. Our stress level went through the roof.

A few days later our oldest son, Josh, awoke with what we thought was a stomach virus. But it didn't subside. Twenty-four hours later he was in the hospital with appendicitis waiting for surgery. We waited...and waited...and waited...for another twenty-four hours. It was the holiday season, and the hospital was short on staff. As the pain intensified, we feared the worst.

I called a surgeon friend, who advised us to rush Josh to another hospital where he would meet us. But by the time the appendix was finally removed, it was gangrenous and had abscessed. His recovery was grueling—he was hooked up to a pump that continually siphoned the infection out of his abdomen—but he was soon back to normal.

All of these events, of course, added additional stress onto what we already felt from our normal schedules. I suppose it gave me the opportunity to see if the principles in this study really work.

If there is one thing I've learned about stress, it's this: You can't eliminate it from your life. It's inevitable. But you can learn to reduce it, manage it, live with it, trust God with it.

Life goes on…My mother-in-law is doing well (how many can boast that they are three-time cancer survivors?), Josh has graduated from high school and left for college, and we continue to hope that Daniel's tumor doesn't return again. Even now he is facing some neurological issues with his spinal cord that remain to be understood completely. And in the midst of this stress we continue to rest in the truth of James 1:2-4, "Consider it pure joy…whenever you face trials of many kinds, because you know that the testing of your faith develops perseverance…that you may be mature and complete, not lacking anything."

May this study help you do the same.

Doug Daily

Stressed-Out

The first step in learning to overcome stress is
gaining a new perspective.

W A R M • U P   15 M I N U T E S

Interview

To get to know others in the group, pair up with
another couple, and take turns interviewing each
other (husbands interviewing husbands and wives
interviewing wives) using the following questions:

- When you hear the word *stress*, what comes to
  mind?

- What is something that caused you stress as a
  teenager?

- What is the most stressful job you have ever had?

- How do you like to unwind after a particularly
  busy or stressful day?

After everyone has been interviewed, introduce your partner to the group, along with one thing you learned about him or her.

Getting Connected

Pass your books around the room, and have each couple write in their names, phone numbers, and e-mail addresses.

_____
NAME, PHONE, AND E-MAIL

_____
NAME, PHONE, AND E-MAIL

_____
NAME, PHONE, AND E-MAIL

_____
NAME, PHONE, AND E-MAIL

_____
NAME, PHONE, AND E-MAIL

_____
NAME, PHONE, AND E-MAIL

_____
NAME, PHONE, AND E-MAIL

BLUEPRINTS   60 MINUTES

Everybody faces some form of stress. Each of us has felt the tension of snarled traffic, an angry boss, disagreement with our spouse, family pressures, unexpected changes in life, and even burned toast. These constant challenges and demands create stress in our lives and marriages. However, stress is more than just a feeling in response to tension—it has the power to affect our overall well-being.

Causes and Effects of Stress

1. In what ways have you seen stress affect a person physically? emotionally? spiritually?

If you have a large group, form smaller groups of about six people to answer the Blueprints questions. Unless otherwise noted, answer the questions in your subgroup. After finishing each section, take time for subgroups to share their answers with the whole group.

2. What effect can stress have on a marriage?

3. What would you say are the main causes of stress in marriage? In your group, create a top-ten list of "stress starters" in marriage.

Responses to Stress

When faced with stress, our natural tendency is to pursue one of three strategies:

- *Fight:* Gut it out; attack the problem; try to make things work at all costs.
- *Flight:* Run; escape; look for ways to avoid uncomfortable feelings.
- *Fright:* Freeze; do nothing; pretend the stress doesn't exist.

As shown in the next question, these three strategies can be seen in a number of different responses.

4. In which of these ways have you responded to stress in the past?

- work harder
- channel or Web surf
- get angry
- withdraw from family and friends
- go shopping
- change eating habits
- change sleeping habits
- smoke or drink
- deny being under pressure
- lose interest in sex
- become unable to concentrate or make a decision
- become preoccupied with a hobby
- gut it out

How effective were these responses in dealing with stress?

5. What are some effective ways you've found for dealing with stress?

6. A unique challenge in managing stress in marriage is often that a husband and wife react to stress differently. With your spouse, select one of the following scenarios, and discuss how each of you would likely respond. Then relate to the group your similarities or differences in your approaches to the scenario you selected.

- Your spouse is sick and requires a lot of care, and you are feeling pressured from other responsibilities as well.

- Your spouse or child demands your attention at a time when you are busy with an important project.

- Your boss wants you to work extra hours and weekends for a few months to complete a special project, leaving little time for you to spend at home.

7. How can understanding the way your spouse responds to stress help alleviate stress in marriage?

A Fresh Perspective

Often we respond to stress by trying to get rid of whatever we think is causing it. But since it is impossible to eliminate all the stress in our lives, we need to gain a fresh perspective on stress. As we look through the Bible during this study, we find many passages that will help us manage stress by thinking differently about it.

8. Read Matthew 6:34 and John 16:33. What does Jesus say about the nature of things that cause stress in our lives? Which of these insights is helpful to you in your current circumstances?

9. What is the difference between feeling stress over your problems or circumstances and becoming stressed-out or distressed?

10. What do the following passages from Psalms tell us we can do when we are feeling the pressure of stress?

- Psalm 4:1

- Psalm 20:1-2, 6-7

- Psalm 42:5

- Psalm 119:143-144

11. Read Romans 5:1-5. In light of these verses, is stress necessarily a bad thing? Why? How might stress help someone grow in faith?

12. What are some ways stress has had a positive impact on your life?

HomeBuilders Principle:
Stress should be viewed as an opportunity to seek God.

What are some ways you have found to reduce stress? Look back at your list of stress starters (question 3, page 17). As a group, brainstorm a list of "stress busters" in response to these stressors. Then, with your spouse, pick a stress buster you want to use this week.

Stress Starters	*Stress Busters*

After completing the Wrap-Up activity, close this session in prayer. Before leaving, Make a Date with your spouse for the HomeBuilders Project for this session.

Make a Date

Make a date with your spouse to meet before the next session to complete the HomeBuilders Project. Your leader will ask at the next session for you to share one aspect of this experience.

DATE

TIME

LOCATION

As a Couple [10 minutes]

Start your date by taking turns telling each other:

- what the most stressful thing was that has happened to you this week, and
- how you are feeling about this study after having gone through the first session.

Individually [20 minutes]

1. Look back over Session One. What was the main thing you got out of this session?

2. What tends to cause stress for you on an ongoing basis (personally and in your marriage)?

3. What effect do the stresses you've identified tend to have on you? on your spouse? on your marriage?

4. When your spouse is under stress, how are you generally affected?

5. What is something your spouse has done for you that has been helpful in alleviating stress?

6. What is something you could do to help alleviate stress in your spouse's life?

7. As you look back over your marriage, what are some ways you've seen stress benefit you as a couple?

Interact as a Couple [30 minutes]

1. Review your answers from the questions in the previous section. Be open, kind, and understanding, as discussing the subject of stress can sometimes be stressful itself!

2. Evaluate your track record in managing stress in your marriage up to this point by talking about:

- what you have done well.
- what needs improvement.

3. Determine a choice—a step or action—you can take to help overcome stress in your marriage this week.

4. Close in prayer. Pray for God's wisdom and guidance in the specific areas that are creating stress in your lives right now.

For Extra Impact

Stress Test: Answer these questions to help you determine more clearly what stresses affect you. On a scale of 1 (no or almost never) to 5 (yes or almost always), circle the appropriate number.

1. I'm frequently late for, or miss, appointments. 5 4 3 2 1

2. My emotions are near the surface
   (anger or tears come easily). 5 4 3 2 1

3. I feel that others control my time. 5 4 3 2 1

4. I find myself engaging in mental
   arguments with others. 5 4 3 2 1

continued on next page

---

5. I feel like I'm always with people and
   am rarely alone.   5 4 3 2 1

6. I wonder when I'm going to get around
   to what I want to do.   5 4 3 2 1

7. I feel tired emotionally, physically, or spiritually.   5 4 3 2 1

8. On my day off, I feel compelled to work.   5 4 3 2 1

9. My spouse and I seem too busy or tired
   for romance.   5 4 3 2 1

10. I think "grass is greener" thoughts
    about my future.   5 4 3 2 1

11. I find myself seeking "escapes"
    (like food, sleep, and TV).   5 4 3 2 1

12. I always feel busy—rushing from
    one thing to the next.   5 4 3 2 1

13. I am not sleeping well.   5 4 3 2 1

14. I'm overly concerned with finances.   5 4 3 2 1

15. I don't have time to maintain my
    most important relationships.   5 4 3 2 1

16. I'm always busy but wonder if
    I'm doing the right things.   5 4 3 2 1

17. I'm dealing with stressful external
    circumstances (such as the birth of a baby,
    a job change, or the loss of someone close).   5 4 3 2 1

                                                TOTAL: ___

Scoring:
     61-85: Running on empty!
     36-60: Medium stress. Make some adjustments.
     17-35: Low stress in general, but address any 4s and 5s.

This test was written by Scott Morton and originally appeared in Discipleship Journal (Issue 110, 1999, p. 28). Reprinted by permission of the author.

Remember to bring your calendar to the next session so you can Make a Date.

Stress From a Hurried Lifestyle

Another key to dealing with stress in marriage is to make wise choices concerning your time and your focus.

W A R M • U P   15 M I N U T E S

Lifestyles of the Stressed and Frazzled

Do you have a case of hurry sickness? Review the following symptoms, placing a check next to the ones you have.

__ I prefer to be first in line at a red light and will change lanes to be so.

__ I always seem to be running just a little late.

__ I rely on my ability to multitask (for example: drive, talk on my cell phone, drink my coffee, and shave or apply make-up, all at the same time).

__ My desk could be declared a disaster area.

__ When I'm in the express lane at the grocery store, I count the number of items in the basket ahead of me.

__ I find myself rushing even when there is no need to rush.

__ I have a hard time saying "no" when people ask me to do things.

__ I have all my important phone numbers on speed dial.

__ I would be lost without my PDA (personal digital assistant) or cell phone by my side.

__ I find myself wishing the microwave would hurry up.

__ I have been known to complain about the service at a fast-food restaurant being too slow.

__ I have to check e-mail at least once a day (including the weekend).

Your score: __ (Give yourself one point for each symptom checked.)

Hurry Scale

1-3 You have a healthy pace in life.

4-6 You have a mild case of hurry sickness.

7-9 You have a full-blown case of hurry sickness.

10-12 You have a terminal case of hurry sickness.

After everyone has determined his or her score, answer these questions:

- What was your score?
- Which symptom did you identify with the most? Why?

Project Report

Share one thing you learned from last session's HomeBuilders Project.

BLUEPRINTS   60 MINUTES

Hurry is the curse of our age. Our lives get so busy with demands at home, at work, volunteering at church and in the community, and trying to be a good neighbor. We rush from one activity to another, looking for ways to do more things in less time, with little thought given to the effect this has on our lives and marriages.

The Hurried Family

Case Study

From the outside, 911 Cliff Drive looked like the place to be. There were two new cars and a fishing boat in the garage, and a new addition was being added to the back of the house. The backyard had all the amenities: a pool and hot tub, a nice deck, and a professionally constructed treehouse. Harry and Henrietta Hurried, the occupants at 911 Cliff Drive, were a bright, successful couple with three children (who all, by the way, arrived *before* their due dates).

Harry was an insurance salesman, and he coached their younger son's fourth-grade basketball team. Henrietta worked six hours a day at a local elementary school and co-led their daughter's Girl Scout troop. In addition, she and Harry took their kids to various practices and lessons—gymnastics, piano, and soccer. Their ninth-grade son was involved in band and school sports. Every game and concert was important, so Harry or Henrietta made almost every one of them.

The Hurrieds were also heavily involved in their church. On Sundays they taught Sunday school and attended worship, and on Wednesday evenings they participated in a HomeBuilders group. When the youth group at church needed a high school sponsor, the Hurrieds were asked. Harry wasn't sure they could make the commitment, but couldn't see how they could say no.

Life in the Hurried house started early and ended late. Harry and Henrietta would collapse in bed exhausted. Before falling asleep, they would briefly talk about the next day's schedule. Weekends didn't provide much of a break, as Saturdays were often spent going to ballgames and shopping or trying to get their boat out to the lake, and Sundays were busy with church and trying to get ready for the week ahead.

Harry and Henrietta both sensed something was wrong with their lifestyle. They felt that they really didn't spend much time with their children outside of shuttling them to different activities, and they weren't as close as they once had been. They were starting to drift apart but didn't know what to do.

If you have a large group, form smaller groups of about six people to answer the Blueprints questions. Unless otherwise noted, answer the questions in your subgroup. After finishing each section, take time for subgroups to share their answers with the whole group.

1. In what ways can you relate to the Hurrieds?

2. What effect do you think the Hurrieds' lifestyle has on their ability to communicate with each other? to love each other?

3. Following are some statements Harry and Henrietta might make to justify their hurried lifestyle:

I know we should spend more time together as a couple...we'll make up for it in the future.

I wish we both didn't have to work, but we need the money.

You can't say "no" to your church. After all, it is the Lord's work.

It is important for children to be involved in lots of activities. It's a competitive world, and they need a variety of experiences if they are to get into a good college and be successful.

How would you evaluate these statements? Pick one statement to respond to. Do you agree? disagree? Explain.

HomeBuilders Principle:
The stress of a hurried lifestyle hurts our ability to love effectively.

A Tale of Two Sisters

What does the Bible say about handling the stress of a hurried lifestyle? One relevant passage tells the story of two sisters and their special guest.

Read Luke 10:38-42.

4. From what you know of Martha in this story, what qualities do you admire in her? What do you admire about Mary?

5. What pressures do you suspect Martha was feeling over having the Son of God as a guest in her home?

6. In the passage we read, Jesus said, "Mary has chosen what is better." What is the "better" thing Mary chose? What made Mary's choice better than Martha's?

7. Who do you tend to be more like, Martha or Mary? Explain.

> **HomeBuilders Principle:**
> *Hurry comes not from a disordered schedule but from a heart disordered by wrong priorities.*

An Ordered Heart

The *first step* to curing a disordered heart is to begin a life of devotion. As you spend time with God, he can give you the wisdom to look critically at your schedule and determine whether your decisions reflect true biblical values.

8. Read Psalm 46:10. What do you think this Psalm intends when it counsels us to "be still"? What are some effective ways you have found to spend time with God?

9. A life of devotion is more than having a daily quiet time. Read 1 Thessalonians 5:17. How do you think your life would change if you were to maintain a "dialogue" with God on a continual basis throughout the day?

A *second step* to curing a disordered heart is to examine the values that drive your schedule.

10. Think again about Harry and Henrietta Hurried. One of the primary reasons their life is so hectic is the number of extracurricular activities in which their children are engaged. In light of what you know about God's Word, what decisions should the Hurrieds make to reduce the stress in their lives from this busyness?

Answer questions 11 and 12 with your spouse. After answering, you may want to share an appropriate insight or discovery with the group.

11. What is one thing in your schedule that you feel is producing too much stress on you, on your spouse, or on your marriage? Does this "stress producer" have to be a part of your schedule? Explain.

12. What is one decision you could make that would reduce the stress in your marriage from a hurried liefstyle?

HomeBuilders Principle:
To bring peace to your marriage, you need to spend time with God.

W R A P • U P   15   M I N U T E S

Psalm 46:10 encourages us to "Be still, and know that I am God." Practice being still before God for five minutes. During this time try to clear your mind of all distractions and focus on God. After the time is up, discuss these questions:

- How hard was it for you to be still physically? spiritually?

- How long did the time seem?

- What thoughts went through your mind as you tried to focus on God?

- What might be the long-term benefits of regularly taking time to be still before God?

Make a Date

Make a date with your spouse to meet before the next session to complete the HomeBuilders Project. Your leader will ask at the next session for you to share one thing from this experience.

_____

DATE

_____

TIME

_____

LOCATION

HOMEBUILDERS PROJECT   60 MINUTES

As a Couple [10 minutes]

Reread the case study starting on page 29. In what ways is your lifestyle similar to the Hurrieds?

Individually [20 minutes]

1. What is one way this session challenged you?

2. What effect is your current pace of life having on you? your spouse? your marriage?

3. In a newspaper column, family psychologist John Rosemond wrote, "A family is people growing together, not people running around like chickens with their heads cut off, trying to meet deadlines and fulfill obligations, most of which are arbitrary. Do you want your children to grow up remembering relaxed family evenings, or do you want them remembering that almost every evening was a 'hurry up, we gotta go!' occasion?"

What is your response to this question?

4. What could you cut from your current schedule to make your life less hurried?

5. Of the choices you have made in the last twenty-four hours, what sticks out as a good choice? a not so good choice?

6. What ultimately unimportant things tend to distract you from priorities that are better? How might you reduce these distractions?

7. What one thing will you do this week to spend time with God?

Interact as a Couple [30 minutes]

1. Share your answers to the individual questions.

2. Discuss what it would take to develop a less hurried lifestyle.

3. Agree on one thing you will do this week to be less busy.

4. To close, read Psalm 46:10, and spend some quiet time before God in prayer.

Remember to bring your calendar to the next session so you can Make a Date.

Putting Work in Its Place

Reducing stress in marriage requires developing and living with a healthy tension between work and other priorities.

W A R M • U P   15   M I N U T E S

My Cup Runneth Over

Once everyone has a cup and rock, form a circle around the pile of household objects. Your goal is to fit as many objects inside your cup (below the rim) as you can, with one condition: You are required to fit your rock in somewhere. After a few minutes, stop and see who was able to get the most objects into his or her cup. Then discuss these questions:

Leader: For this Warm-Up, each person will need a plastic or Styrofoam cup and a rock that will fit in the cup, taking up at least half of the space inside. You will also need an assortment of household objects that can fit inside the cup—coins, buttons, nails, spools of thread, pieces of cloth, marbles, or whatever is convenient.

• What is the big thing—the rock—that takes up most of your time in an ordinary day?

- How would you compare this exercise to the struggle we face in deciding how many other things we can squeeze into a day that is taken up mostly by one thing?

Project Report

Share one thing you learned from last session's HomeBuilders Project.

BLUEPRINTS   60 MINUTES

Job Sharing

If you have a large group, form smaller groups of about six people to answer the Blueprints questions. Unless otherwise noted, answer the questions in your subgroup. After finishing each section, take time for subgroups to share their answers with the whole group.

1. Briefly explain the daily responsibilities of your job. What about your job do you like the most? the least?

2. What kinds of things cause you the most stress in your job?

Life in Tension

Work is an essential priority in the life of a married couple. The Bible indicates that work is a blessing from God. Adam was assigned by God to work in the Garden of Eden before the fall (Genesis 2:15). But because of sin, work doesn't yield all we hope it would (Genesis 3:17-19). The result: Work can be stressful!

3. What do you consider to be the most important priorities in your life? Take a minute to write these down, and then share them with the group.

4. When asked to rank their priorities in order of importance, Christians often list their priorities like this:

1) God
2) family
3) work
4) church

- What can be impractical with a list like this?

- How might living life in tension between differing priorities be like training for a triathalon?

5. A biblical view of priorities is less complicated. Read Matthew 6:33 and Mark 12:28-30.

- What priorities do you find in Jesus' words?

- What guidance can we take from these passages concerning the daily choices we make about the other priorities in our lives?

6. Read the passage that follow. What perspective do these verses give about work?

- Ecclesiastes 3:9-13

- Ephesians 4:28

- 1 Thessalonians 4:11-12

- 2 Thessalonians 3:6-13

HomeBuilders Principle:
Life is lived in tension between competing priorities; however, in all we do, we should "seek first his kingdom."

Work and Stress

For many people, work consumes more time than any other commitment. While work is important, it shouldn't rule our lives.

7. In our culture, do you think people generally place too much or too little emphasis on work? Explain.

8. What would you identify as the biggest ways work can cause stress for a married couple?

9. What are some ways you have felt stress from work in your home? in your marriage?

10. Read Ecclesiastes 4:9-12. In what ways do you think teamwork in marriage can help you manage stress at work?

Answer questions 11 and 12 with your spouse. After answering, you may want to share an appropriate insight or discovery with the group.

11. What is the biggest challenge or greatest source of stress from work that you are dealing with right now?

12. What effect is work-related stress having on you? your spouse? your marriage?

HomeBuilders Principle:
Much of the stress we feel about work is the result of unwise choices about the importance of work in our lives.

W R A P • U P   15   M I N U T E S

In thinking about the coming week, what are the top-three things you would like to accomplish at work? What are the top-three things you would like to accomplish in your marriage? List these.

Work	*Marriage*
1.	1.
2.	2.
3.	3.

After recording your goals, share them with your spouse, and discuss how both lists can be achieved.

Make a Date

Make a date with your spouse to meet before the next session to complete the HomeBuilders Project. Your leader will ask at the next session for you to share one thing from this experience.

_____
DATE

_____
TIME

_____
LOCATION

As a Couple [10 minutes]

We all have 168 hours to spend each week. Do the best you can to recap your last week by filling out the following weekly time sheet. For each category, enter your best estimate of how much time you spent over the last week.

__ work (your primary job—include getting ready and commuting time)

__ sleep (include getting ready for bed)

__ exercise

__ other work (things like household chores)

__ TV or computer (personal Web surfing, e-mail)

__ marriage (time spent with your spouse)

__ family/friends (time spent with kids, extended family, and friends)

__ God (include Bible study, prayer, and time at church)

__ errands/shopping

__ meals (include preparation time)

__ other: _____

Total: 168 hours

After you have both completed your time sheets, discuss the following:

- What did you spend too much time doing? too little time doing?

- If you were to trade the amount of time you spent at work with the amount of time you spent on your marriage, what would be the result at work? in your marriage?

Individually [20 minutes]

1. What new or renewed insight or perspective about work and stress did you gain from this session?

2. When it comes to your job, would you say you tend to work too much, too little, or just enough? How would you answer this question for your spouse?

3. What negative consequences do your work habits have on your marriage?

4. What do you like best about your spouse's job? What is one thing you would like to see change about your spouse's job?

5. In what ways does your marriage benefit from the work your spouse does?

6. How could you be more supportive of your spouse in his or her work? What is something your spouse can do to support or encourage you in your work?

7. Related to the amount of stress you have from work, where do you see the career path you are currently on leading? Under what circumstances would you consider a change in career?

Interact as a Couple [30 minutes]

1. Talk through your answers to the individual questions.

2. Brainstorm several ways you could reduce stress from work in your marriage.

3. Decide on one step you will take this week to reduce stress from work in your marriage.

4. Close in prayer with each of you completing this sentence: "Dear God, my prayer for our marriage is…"

Remember to bring your calendar to the next session so you can Make a Date.

Money Matters

Another key to overcoming stress in marriage is to maintain a proper attitude toward money.

W A R M • U P   15 M I N U T E S

Loose Change

Check your pockets or pocketbook for coins. As a group, determine how much money you have collectively in change. Then discuss the following with your spouse:

- Spending up to but not exceeding the amount of change the group has, what is something you could do for a "date"?

Share your idea with the group.

After each couple has had the opportunity to share their idea for a "cheap date," everyone should select one coin at random and answer this question:

- Look at the date on your coin. What is a financial need or want you can remember having in that year?

Project Report

Share one thing you learned from last session's HomeBuilders Project.

BLUEPRINTS   **6o MINUTES**

We go to school to be equipped to earn it. We work forty, fifty, sixty hours a week to have it. We worry about not having enough of it. Marriages fracture over it. And we invest countless hours devising new ways to spend it.

Of course the subject is money. There are few issues that cause more stress in marriage than money.

A Major $ource of $tress

If you have a large group, form smaller groups of about six people to answer the Blueprints questions. Unless otherwise noted, answer the questions in your subgroup. After finishing each section, take time for subgroups to share their answers with the whole group.

1. What was the last major purchase you made as a couple? How stressful was it? Why?

2. What perspective or attitude did you have about money

- as a teenager?
- as a newlywed?

How has your perspective changed from then to now?

3. Money is often cited as a major source of stress in marriages. Why do you think this is?

4. What are some common financial issues that couples face?

Perspectives on Money

When it comes to money and stress, attitude is everything! Money is a powerful commodity. It has the ability to affect our sense of well-being, our self-esteem, and even our joy in life. Money has power far beyond its ability to purchase goods and services.

5. Read Luke 12:13-15. What attitude about money does Jesus warn us about? How much of a problem is this attitude in our culture? Explain.

6. In what way does our culture encourage us to be greedy—to acquire or possess more things than we really need?

7. Read Luke 12:16-21.

- How do you think the man in this parable would be perceived in the business community today? How might his colleagues describe him?

• Why does God call the man in the parable a fool?

• When have you been most like the man in the story—being fooled into thinking an accumulation of "things" could bring you contentment and security?

8. How can false perceptions about money or possessions lead to stress in a marriage?

HomeBuilders Principle:
Wrong attitudes about money lead to bad decisions.

Call to Contentment

Living in a materialistic culture, many people find themselves discontented because they want what they don't have, and they have what they no longer want.

9. When is a time you became preoccupied with acquiring something you just had to have?

10. Read the following passages. What insights regarding money do these verses give us?

- Ecclesiastes 5:10-12

- Luke 12:22-31

- Philippians 4:10-13

- Hebrews 13:5

Answer questions 11 and 12 with your spouse. After answering, you may want to share an appropriate insight or discovery with the group.

11. What are some specific ways money has caused stress in your marriage?

12. What is one of your biggest financial concerns at this time? What have you learned that might help you deal with it?

HomeBuilders Principle:
The key to relieving stress about finances is being content with the resources God has provided for you.

W R A P • U P   15   M I N U T E S

What is an investment you can make with your money that would benefit your marriage? As a group come up with a list of investment opportunities (both short-term and long-term). Then get with your spouse and discuss which investment idea you would like to add to your marriage portfolio.

Make a Date

Make a date with your spouse to meet before the next session to complete the HomeBuilders Project. Your leader will ask at the next session for you to share one thing from this experience.

DATE

TIME

LOCATION

HOMEBUILDERS PROJECT   6 0   M I N U T E S

As a Couple [10 minutes]

How well do you know your spouse? If your spouse received a surprise check for a thousand dollars in the mail, what would he or she likely do? Before sharing, take a minute to record two things in your book:

- what you would do:

- what you predict your spouse would do:

Reveal your plan and prediction, then discuss this question:

- If you were to use your thousand dollars for a weekend away together, what plans would you make?

Individually [20 minutes]

1. What did this session reveal to you—good or bad—about your perspective on money and its effect on your marriage?

2. We often spend money without giving a lot of thought to its impact on our marriage. This assessment is designed to help you recognize financial weaknesses you should address to improve the financial health of your marriage. Answer each question either "yes" or "no."

	Yes	No
• Are your finances a consistent source of tension in your marriage relationship?		
• Do you often feel as if you are living from paycheck to paycheck?		
• Are you unable to save money on a consistent basis?		
• Are you unable to stick to a budget?		
• Are you unaware of what your monthly expenses tend to be for major expenses such as housing, food, gas/auto, and utilities?		
• Are you unable to control spending on frivolous items?		

	Yes	No
• Do you often argue about finances?		
• Do you feel pressure from mounting credit card debt?		
• Do you have to take out loans to pay off debt?		
• Do you have a difficult time talking with your spouse about finances?		
• Do you feel in the dark about your finances because your spouse doesn't give you enough information about what's going on?		
• Do you feel frustrated because you aren't making charitable contributions at the level you would like?		
• Do you feel tension because your spouse has different priorities for where to spend money than you do?		

Review your answers, highlighting problem areas you would like to discuss with your spouse. If you answered "yes" to the majority of the assessment questions, you may want to talk with your spouse about seeking professional financial advice or counseling.

3. Which areas in the assessment exercise did you highlight? What are one or two steps you could take to begin to improve these areas?

4. As you look back over your years together, what have been some of your biggest successes and your biggest mistakes in handling finances?

5. In what ways can you tie these successes and mistakes to your level of contentment and trust in God's provision for you?

6. How do you and your spouse complement one another in how you handle your finances?

Interact as a Couple [30 minutes]

1. Discuss and compare your responses to the previous questions. Keep your focus positive, as there can be a tendency to place blame when discussing finances.

2. Review all your expenditures over the last twenty-four hours. Talk over the impact these spending decisions had on your finances and on your marriage. What was good? What could have been better?

3. Money moves in four directions: You can spend it, save (invest) it, give it away, or pay debt. Talk about these four areas.

- What kind of balance would you like to have between these areas? How would this reduce stress from money in your marriage?
- Which area causes you the most stress in your marriage? What would it take to start moving toward the balance you want?

4. Read Psalm 20:7. What is a choice you can make this week to trust God with your finances? Pray, asking God to help you as you seek to reduce stress from money in your marriage.

Remember to bring your calendar to the next session so you can Make a Date.

Stress From Family Relationships

To reduce the marital stress that comes from family relationships, we should practice peacemaking.

W A R M • U P   15   M I N U T E S

Strings Attached

Once everyone has five pieces of string, form groups of up to six people. Each group should stand in a circle with a diameter of about six feet. The challenge of this exercise is for you to quickly become connected to everyone in your circle. When your leader says "Go!" everyone should simultaneously attempt to connect with everyone else in the circle as quickly as possible by running a separate length of string between you and each person in your circle. It doesn't matter if the strings get tangled, as long as

Leader: For this Warm-Up, each person will need five lengths of string, twine, or yarn, approximately six feet in length.

everyone is connected. After everyone is connected, discuss these questions:

- What difficulties did you face in trying to connect with the others in your circle?
- If one person were to fall down or try to walk away while still holding all of his or her strings, what effect would it have on your connection? on your group's connection?
- How is this exercise like trying to stay connected to your spouse and family?

Project Report

Share one thing you learned from last session's HomeBuilders Project.

BLUEPRINTS 60 MINUTES

The Strain of Family Relationships

Relationship problems, particularly in a family, can be a major contributor of stress in our lives. You can employ a dozen successful strategies for handling stress in this area, but none of them will ultimately be effective if an unresolved conflict exists.

1. Which of the following family relationships tend to cause stress for you?

If you have a large group,
form smaller groups of
about six people to
answer the Blueprints
questions. Unless other-
wise noted, answer the
questions in your
subgroup. After finishing
each section, take time
for subgroups to share
their answers with the
whole group.

- parents
- in-laws
- children
- siblings
- other: _____

2. In what ways does stress from the relationship you
identified in the previous question affect your marriage?

3. As a child, what was the most common method of
handling family conflict that you observed in your
home?

4. How do you generally respond to conflict?

The Value of Resolving Conflict

5. When a conflict, especially between family members, is left unresolved, what are some of the consequences?

6. Read Ephesians 4:26-27. How do you think unresolved anger can "give the devil a foothold"?

7. Now read Matthew 5:9. Why do you think Jesus calls peacemakers "blessed"? In your experience, what are good strategies people use to try to make peace? bad strategies people use?

8. What does Matthew 5:21-25 tell us about resolving conflict? Why do you suppose Jesus said, "If you...remember that your brother has something against you" rather than, "If you remember you have something against your brother"?

9. Read Colossians 3:12-15 for additional counsel on resolving conflict. In what ways should God's forgiveness be a model for us as we forgive others?

10. What is a current situation in your family that needs to be resolved? How could you initiate peace in this situation?

Answer question 10 with your spouse. After answering, you may want to share an appropriate insight or discovery with the group.

HomeBuilders Principle:
God wants us to be peacemakers to take the initiative in resolving conflict.

Creating a Safe Zone

One of the best ways to reduce stress and improve communication in your family is to make your home a safe zone. A safe zone is a place where time is taken to talk and to actively listen, with the goal of understanding.

Case Study

Narrator: When Rod arrived home from work, he could tell that his wife, Cindy, was discouraged.

Rod: (concerned) Hi, honey. Rough day?

Cindy: (tired and a little emotional) Yeah, nothing went right today.

Narrator: After dinner and helping the kids with their homework, Rod and Cindy sat down to talk.

Rod: So, tell me about your day. What can I do to help?

Cindy: (frustrated) I feel like a taxi driver, shuffling children all over town. And what's worse, I don't get paid. Nobody even says thank you! Just today I had to make two extra trips to Shane's school and one to Annie's. First Shane forgot his lunch, and then he called because he didn't have his basketball shoes. That made me late to my women's Bible study, and right in the middle of the fellowship time, I remembered I'd promised Annie that I'd drop a check by the school office for gymnastics. It's like everyone expects good old mom to pick up all the loose ends.

Narrator: Rod starts to speak, but Cindy continues.

Cindy: And that wasn't even the worst of it. *Your* parents called today and said they want us to come for Thanksgiving. I told them we wouldn't be able to this year. Naturally, they weren't happy. I'm getting tired of the way they try to make us feel guilty every time we don't do what they want. When I suggested that they come here for Thanksgiving, they said, "But we've always done it here—it just wouldn't be the same." Rod, *you* have to talk to them!

Rod: (in a matter-of-fact tone) Well, first of all, you shouldn't feel obligated to pick up the loose ends for Shane. I really think you might be mothering him too much. He's fourteen, and it's

OK for him to face the consequences of his forgetfulness. I'll talk to him about being more responsible.

And I really think you should take a few minutes before bed to plan the next day. I spend the first twenty minutes at work planning my day, and it really helps. I think I have an extra day planner at the office. I'll bring one home for you. And feel free to call me. Even though my day is usually pretty full, I can break away at times to run something to the kids.

As for my parents, you know it's better for me to bring up the holidays with them. You should have waited to tell them about Thanksgiving. And I know you always feel like we let them get their way, but what are we supposed to do?

Cindy: (rising and walking away) Well, you just have an answer for everything!

11. How do you think Rod should have acted with Cindy?

12. How might this situation change if the roles were reversed?

WRAP • UP   15 MINUTES

Case Study (Epilogue)

Rod was surprised by Cindy's response. After all, he
thought his advice was pretty good. But as he sat in the
living room reflecting on what had just transpired, he
thought, "I didn't really try to understand Cindy. I just
wanted to solve the problems and get on with life."

In separate groups of men and women, revisit the
Rod and Cindy case study. In each group discuss
what should happen next. After each group has
determined what Rod and Cindy should do, present
your scenario (in dramatic fashion if you'd like).
Then discuss:

- What was different about Rod and Cindy's
  exchange as presented by your groups compared
  to their first exchange?

Make a Date

Make a date with your spouse to meet before the next
session to complete the HomeBuilders Project. Your

leader will ask at the next session for you to share one thing from this experience.

DATE

TIME

LOCATION

HOMEBUILDERS PROJECT   6 0   M I N U T E S

As a Couple [10 minutes]

Think about your relationship with the members of your family, concentrating first on the members of your immediate family but also including your extended family as time permits. Describe to your spouse in terms of the weather how you are feeling about each relationship. For example, you might say, "About our oldest son, I'm feeling like it's partly cloudy with a chance of rain." Take turns sharing weather reports.

Individually [20 minutes]

1. What insight or concept from this session do you want to apply to your life?

2. To begin applying what you identified in the previous question, what initial step can you take?

3. As you think about your relationships with family members, which are you most concerned about? What stress or conflict have you had lately with family?

4. In these relationships, how is conflict between you and the other person usually resolved? How effective have your conflict-resolution efforts been? Why?

5. What steps are you willing to take to initiate peacemaking? Be specific.

6. When an issue or conflict comes between you and your spouse, how willing would you say you generally are to initiate peace when you have been offended? when you are the offender?

7. What would you like to see change in the way you and your spouse handle stress in family relationships?

Interact as a Couple [30 minutes]

1. Go over the questions you answered individually.

2. Talk about how you can create a safe zone for dealing with conflict or stressful issues.

3. Read Romans 12:9-18. Discuss how these verses could be applied to relationships that cause stress in your marriage.

4. Pray, asking God to help you in your pursuit of peace.

Remember to bring your calendar to the next session so you can Make a Date.

Stress From Hardships

Stress from the hardships of life can drive a couple
apart unless they recognize the trials as an
opportunity to draw closer to God.

W A R M • U P   15   M I N U T E S

Hard Times

Choose one of the following questions to answer and
share with the group:

- How many broken bones have you had?
- Who is better in a crisis, you or your spouse?
  Why?
- What was the first big crisis (serious or funny)
  you faced in your marriage?

Project Report

Share one thing you learned from last session's
HomeBuilders Project.

At some point, everybody faces serious hardships, and often they are beyond our control. A serious hardship or trial can come at any time and take on a number of different forms. It may be a devastating medical diagnosis, a child with learning disabilities, an injury from an accident, or the death of a loved one. If we don't handle hardships well, they can raise our level of stress and wedge us apart as couples.

When the Going Gets Tough

If you have a large group, form smaller groups of about six people to answer the Blueprints questions. Unless otherwise noted, answer the questions in your subgroup. After finishing each section, take time for subgroups to share their answers with the whole group.

1. When trouble hits or bad things happen, how do you tend to react or respond?

2. Why do you think many couples are driven apart by serious hardships? What are the common mistakes they make?

3. Think about a serious hardship you have faced in your marriage. How has this hardship affected

Answer question 3 with your spouse. After answering, you may want to share an appropriate insight or discovery with the group.

- your relationship with each other?
- your relationship with God?

A Biblical Perspective on Hardships

Hardships cannot be avoided. However, the amount of stress we experience from them and how we deal with that stress depends on how we view the trials we face.

Read James 1:2-4, 12.

4. What do you think James means when he tells us to "Consider it pure joy...whenever you face trials"? How can we do that?

5. According to James 1:3-4, 12, what benefits can trials or hardships bring?

HomeBuilders Principle:
God works through hardships to mature and complete us in our faith.

Help in Hardships

Read James 1:2-8.

6. In what context does James instruct us to ask God for wisdom? Practically, how can we ask for and receive wisdom from God?

7. Read the following passages:

- Psalm 34:8-10
- Psalm 52:8-9
- Psalm 100:4-5
- Romans 8:28, 35-39

Why are these biblical truths important for us to believe in the midst of hardship?

8. In James 1:6 we are instructed when asking God for wisdom to "believe and not doubt." What are some ways we are inclined to doubt God in the midst of hardships?

9. What are the consequences of asking for wisdom while doubting God?

10. If you can, tell the group about a time you debated with God or had doubts about his goodness and love during a severe hardship. How did the debate end?

11. Read Philippians 4:6-7. When is a time you experienced God's peace in the midst of a trial as a result of putting this passage into practice?

12. When have you experienced God's peace in the midst of difficult circumstances? How did that affect your faith?

HomeBuilders Principle:
Hardships test our faith, providing opportunities to draw closer to God.

W R A P • U P   15   M I N U T E S

As you come to the end of this course, take a few minutes to reflect on this experience. Review the following questions, and write down responses to the questions you can answer. Then relate to the group one or more of your answers.

• What has this group meant to you over the course of this study? Be specific.

- What is the most valuable thing that you have learned or discovered?

- How have you, or your marriage, been changed or challenged?

- What would you like to see happen next for this group?

Make a Date

Make a date with your spouse to meet in the next week to complete the last HomeBuilders Project of this study.

DATE

TIME

LOCATION

As a Couple [10 minutes]

Congratulations—you have made it to the last project of this course! Start your date by reflecting on the dates you have had throughout this study and their impact on your marriage.

Part of overcoming stress in your marriage is an ongoing commitment to know and understand each other better. A good way to do this is to continue the practice of setting aside time to spend together. Take a few minutes to schedule and plan another date—one without homework!

Individually [20 minutes]

1. How has this session on stress from hardships challenged you?

2. What hardship are you currently facing? Take a few minutes to pray about this situation, asking God for wisdom.

3. Overall, what has been the most important insight or lesson for you from this course?

4. What expectations did you have going into this study on stress? How did your experience compare to your expectations?

5. This study focused on five contributors to stress in marriage: lifestyle, work, money, family, and hardships. How would you rank these from 1 to 5, with 1 being the smallest contributor to stress in your marriage and 5 being the greatest?

___ lifestyle
___ work
___ money
___ family
___ hardships

6. What can be done to reduce stress from what you identified as the top contributor?

7. Looking back, what action or step that you identified during this course do you need to follow up on?

Interact as a Couple [30 minutes]

1. Review and discuss your responses to the previous questions.

2. Make a list of the most significant trials you have faced together in the years you have been married.

Following is a list of some of the benefits of trials:

- strengthen our relationship with God
- force us to depend on grace
- bind us together with others
- produce discernment
- foster sensitivity
- discipline our minds
- spend our time wisely
- stretch our hope
- lead us to repentance of sin
- strengthen our characters
- teach us to give thanks
- draw us closer as a couple

What benefits—from the list or others—have you experienced from the hardships you've faced?

_____

3. Evaluate things you should continue to do to strengthen your marriage. You may want to consider continuing the practice of regularly setting aside time as you have for these projects. You may also want to look at the ideas on page 87 in "Where Do You Go From Here?"

4. Close in prayer. Thank God for each other, and pray for his wisdom, direction, and blessing in your marriage.

Please visit our Web site at www.familylife.com/homebuilders to give us your feedback on this study and to get information on other FamilyLife resources and conferences.

OVERCOMING STRESS IN YOUR MARRIAGE

Where Do You Go From Here?

It is our prayer that you have benefited greatly from this study in the HomeBuilders Couples Series. We hope that your marriage will continue to grow as you both submit your lives to Jesus Christ and build according to his blueprints.

We also hope that you will begin reaching out to strengthen other marriages in your community and local church. Your church needs couples like you who are committed to building Christian marriages. A favorite World War II story illustrates this point very clearly.

The year was 1940. The French Army had just collapsed under Hitler's onslaught. The Dutch had folded, overwhelmed by the Nazi regime. The Belgians had surrendered. And the British Army was trapped on the coast of France in the channel port of Dunkirk.

Two hundred and twenty thousand of Britain's finest young men seemed doomed to die, turning the English Channel red with their blood. The Fuehrer's troops, only miles away in the hills of France, didn't realize how close to victory they actually were.

Any rescue seemed feeble and futile in the time remaining. A "thin" British Navy—"the professionals"—told King George VI that at best they could save 17,000 troops. The House of Commons was warned to prepare for "hard and heavy tidings."

Politicians were paralyzed. The king was powerless. And the Allies could only watch as spectators from a distance. Then as the doom of the British Army seemed imminent, a strange fleet appeared on the horizon of the English Channel—the wildest assortment of boats perhaps ever assembled in history.

Trawlers, tugs, scows, fishing sloops, lifeboats, pleasure craft, smacks and coasters, sailboats, even the London fire-brigade flotilla. *Each ship was manned by civilian volunteers—English fathers sailing to rescue Britain's exhausted, bleeding sons.*

William Manchester writes in his epic book, *The Last Lion*, that even today what happened in 1940 in less than twenty-four hours seems like a miracle—not only were all of the British soldiers rescued, but 118,000 other Allied troops as well.

Today the Christian home is much like those troops at Dunkirk. Pressured, trapped, and demoralized, it needs help. Your help. The Christian community may be much like England—we stand waiting for politicians, professionals, even for our pastors to step in and save the family. But the problem is much larger than all of those combined can solve.

With the highest divorce rate of any nation on earth, we need an all-out effort by men and women "sailing" to rescue the exhausted and wounded family casualties. We need an outreach effort by common couples with faith in an uncommon God. For too long, married couples within the church have abdicated the privilege and responsibility of influencing others to those in full-time vocational ministry.

Possibly this study has indeed been used to "light the torch" of your spiritual lives. Perhaps it was already burning, and this provided more fuel. Regardless, may we challenge you to invest your lives in others?

You and other couples around the world can team together to build thousands of marriages and families. By starting a HomeBuilders group, you will not only strengthen other marriages but you will also see your marriage grow as you share these principles with others.

Will You Join Us in "Touching Lives...Changing Families"?

The following are some practical ways you can make a difference in families today:

1. Gather a group of four to eight couples, and lead them through the six sessions of this HomeBuilders study, *Overcoming Stress in Your Marriage*. (Why not consider challenging others in your church or community to form additional HomeBuilders groups?)

2. Commit to continue marriage building by doing another course in the HomeBuilders Couples Series.

3. An excellent outreach tool is the film *"JESUS,"* which is available on video. For more information, contact FamilyLife at 1-800-FL-TODAY.

4. Host a dinner party. Invite families from your neighborhood to your home, and as a couple share your faith in Christ.

5. Reach out and share the love of Christ with neighborhood children.

6. If you have attended the FamilyLife Marriage Conference, why not offer to assist your pastor in counseling couples engaged to be married, using the material you received?

For more information about any of the above ministry opportunities, contact your local church, or write:

> **FamilyLife**
> P.O. Box 8220
> Little Rock, AR 72221-8220
> 1-800-FL-TODAY
> **www.familylife.com**

Our Problems, God's Answers

Every couple eventually has to deal with problems in marriage. Communication problems. Money problems. Difficulties with sexual intimacy. These issues are important to cultivating a strong, loving relationship with your spouse. The HomeBuilders Couples Series is designed to help you strengthen your marriage in many of these critical areas.

Part One: The Big Problem

One basic problem is at the heart of every other problem in every marriage, and it's a problem we can't help you fix. No matter how hard you try, this is one problem that is too big for you to deal with on your own.

The problem is separation from God. If you want to experience marriage the way it was designed to be, you need a vital relationship with the God who created you and offers you the power to live a life of joy and purpose.

And what separates us from God is one more problem—sin. Most of us have assumed throughout our lives that the term "sin" refers to a list of bad habits that everyone agrees are wrong. We try to deal with our sin problem by working hard to become better people. We read books to learn how to control our anger, or we resolve to stop cheating on our taxes.

But in our hearts, we know our sin problem runs much deeper than a list of bad habits. All of us have rebelled against God. We have ignored him and have decided to run our own lives in a way that makes sense to us. The Bible says that the God who created us wants us to follow his plan for our lives. But because of our sin problem, we think our ideas and plans are better than his.

- *"For all have sinned and fall short of the glory of God"* (Romans 3:23).

What does it mean to "fall short of the glory of God"? It means that none of us has trusted and treasured God the way we should. We have sought to satisfy ourselves with other things and have treated those things as more valuable than God. We have gone our own way. According to the Bible, we have to pay a penalty for our sin. We cannot simply do things the way we choose and hope it will all be OK with God. Following our own plan leads to our destruction.

- *"There is a way that seems right to a man, but in the end it leads to death"* (Proverbs 14:12).

- *"For the wages of sin is death"* (Romans 6:23a).

The penalty for sin is that we are forever separated from God's love. God is holy, and we are sinful. No matter how hard we try, we cannot come up with some plan, like living a good life or even trying to do what the Bible says, and hope that we can avoid the penalty.

God's Solution to Sin

Thankfully, God has a way to solve our dilemma. He became a man through the person of Jesus Christ. He lived a holy life, in perfect obedience to God's plan. He also willingly died on a cross to pay our penalty for sin. Then he proved that he is more powerful than sin or death by rising from the dead. He alone has the power to overrule the penalty for our sin.

- *"Jesus answered, 'I am the way and the truth and the life. No one comes to the Father except through me'"* (John 14:6).

- *"But God demonstrates his own love for us in this: While we were still sinners, Christ died for us"* (Romans 5:8).

- *"Christ died for our sins...he was buried...he was raised on the third day according to the Scriptures...he appeared to Peter, and then to the Twelve. After that, he appeared to more than five hundred"* (1 Corinthians 15:3-6).

- *"For the wages of sin is death, but the gift of God is eternal life in Christ Jesus our Lord"* (Romans 6:23).

The death of Jesus has fixed our sin problem. He has bridged the gap between God and us. He is calling all of us to come to him and to give up our own flawed plan for how to run our lives. He wants us to trust God and his plan.

Accepting God's Solution

If you agree that you are separated from God, he is calling you to confess your sins. All of us have made messes of our lives because we have stubbornly preferred our ideas and plans over his. As a result, we deserve to be cut off from God's love and his care for us. But God has promised that if we will agree that we have rebelled against his plan for us and have messed up our lives, he will forgive us and will fix our sin problem.

- *"Yet to all who received him, to those who believed in his name, he gave the right to become children of God"* (John 1:12).

- *"For it is by grace you have been saved, through faith—and this not from yourselves, it is the gift of*

God—not by works, so that no one can boast"
(Ephesians 2:8-9).

When the Bible talks about receiving Christ, it means we acknowledge that we are sinners and that we can't fix the problem ourselves. It means we turn away from our sin. And it means we trust Christ to forgive our sins and to make us the kind of people he wants us to be. It's not enough to just intellectually believe that Christ is the Son of God. We must trust in him and his plan for our lives by faith, as an act of the will.

Are things right between you and God, with him and his plan at the center of your life? Or is life spinning out of control as you seek to make your way on your own?

You can decide today to make a change. You can turn to Christ and allow him to transform your life. All you need to do is to talk to him and tell him what is stirring in your mind and in your heart. If you've never done this before, consider taking the steps listed here:

- Do you agree that you need God? Tell God.

- Have you made a mess of your life by following your own plan? Tell God.

- Do you want God to forgive you? Tell God.

- Do you believe that Jesus' death on the cross and his resurrection from the dead gave him the power to fix your sin problem and to grant you the gift of eternal life? Tell God.

- Are you ready to acknowledge that God's plan for your life is better than any plan you could come up with? Tell God.

- Do you agree that God has the right to be the Lord and master of your life? Tell God.

"Seek the Lord while he may be found;
call on him while he is near"
(Isaiah 55:6).

Following is a suggested prayer:

Lord Jesus, I need you. Thank you for dying on the
cross for my sins. I receive you as my Savior and Lord.
Thank you for forgiving my sins and giving me eternal
life. Make me the kind of person you want me to be.

Does this prayer express the desire of your heart? If it
does, pray it right now, and Christ will come into your life, as
he promised.

Part Two: Living the Christian Life

For a person who is a follower of Christ—a Christian—the
penalty for sin is paid in full. But the effect of sin continues
throughout our lives.

- *"If we claim to be without sin, we deceive ourselves*
  and the truth is not in us" (1 John 1:8).

- *"For what I do is not the good I want to do; no,*
  the evil I do not want to do—this I keep on doing"
  (Romans 7:19).

The effects of sin carry over into our marriages as well.
Even Christians struggle to maintain solid, God-honoring marriages. Most couples eventually realize that they can't do it on
their own. But with God's help, they can succeed. The Holy
Spirit can have a huge impact in the marriages of Christians
who live constantly, moment by moment, under his gracious
direction.

Self-Centered Christians

Many Christians struggle to live the Christian life in their own strength because they are not allowing God to control their lives. Their interests are self-directed, often resulting in failure and frustration.

- *"Brothers, I could not address you as spiritual but as worldly—mere infants in Christ. I gave you milk, not solid food, for you were not yet ready for it. Indeed, you are still not ready. You are still worldly. For since there is jealousy and quarreling among you, are you not worldly? Are you not acting like mere men?"* (1 Corinthians 3:1-3).

The self-centered Christian cannot experience the abundant and fruitful Christian life. Such people trust in their own efforts to live the Christian life: They are either uninformed about—or have forgotten—God's love, forgiveness, and power. This kind of Christian

- has an up-and-down spiritual experience.

- cannot understand himself—he wants to do what is right, but cannot.

- fails to draw upon the power of the Holy Spirit to live the Christian life.

Some or all of the following traits may characterize the Christian who does not fully trust God:

disobedience	plagued by impure thoughts
lack of love for God and others	jealous
	worrisome
inconsistent prayer life	easily discouraged, frustrated
lack of desire for Bible study	critical
legalistic attitude	lack of purpose

Note: The individual who professes to be a Christian but who continues to practice sin should realize that he may not be a Christian at all, according to Ephesians 5:5 and 1 John 2:3; 3:6, 9.

Spirit-Centered Christians

When a Christian puts Christ on the throne of his life, he yields to God's control. This Christian's interests are directed by the Holy Spirit, resulting in harmony with God's plan.

- *"But the fruit of the Spirit is love, joy, peace, patience, kindness, goodness, faithfulness, gentleness and self-control. Against such things there is no law"* (Galatians 5:22-23).

Jesus said:

- *"I have come that they may have life, and have it to the full"* (John 10:10b).

- *"I am the vine; you are the branches. If a man remains in me and I in him, he will bear much fruit; apart from me you can do nothing"* (John 15:5).

- *"But you will receive power when the Holy Spirit comes on you; and you will be my witnesses in Jerusalem, and in all Judea and Samaria, and to the ends of the earth"* (Acts 1:8).

The following traits result naturally from the Holy Spirit's work in our lives:

Christ centered	love
Holy Spirit empowered	joy
motivated to tell others about Jesus	peace
	patience
dedicated to prayer	kindness
student of God's Word	goodness
trusts God	faithfulness
obeys God	gentleness
	self-control

The degree to which these traits appear in a Christian's life and marriage depends upon the extent to which the Christian trusts the Lord with every detail of life, and upon that person's maturity in Christ. One who is only beginning to understand the ministry of the Holy Spirit should not be discouraged if he is not as fruitful as mature Christians who have known and experienced this truth for a longer period of time.

Giving God Control

Jesus promises his followers an abundant and fruitful life as they allow themselves to be directed and empowered by the Holy Spirit. As we give God control of our lives, Christ lives in and through us in the power of the Holy Spirit (John 15).

If you sincerely desire to be directed and empowered by God, you can turn your life over to the control of the Holy Spirit right now (Matthew 5:6; John 7:37-39).

First, confess your sins to God, agreeing with him that you want to turn from any past sinful patterns in your life. Thank God in faith that he has forgiven all of your sins because Christ died for you (Colossians 2:13-15; 1 John 1:9; 2:1-3; Hebrews 10:1-18).

Be sure to offer every area of your life to God (Romans 12:1-2). Consider what areas you might rather keep to yourself, and be sure you're willing to give God control in those areas.

By faith, commit yourself to living according to the Holy Spirit's guidance and power.

- *Live by the Spirit:* **"So I say, live by the Spirit, and you will not gratify the desires of the sinful nature. For the sinful nature desires what is contrary to the Spirit, and the Spirit what is contrary to the sinful nature. They are in conflict with each other, so that you do not do what you want"** (Galatians 5:16-17).

- *Trust in God's promise:* **"This is the confidence we have in approaching God: that if we ask anything according to his will, he hears us. And if we know that he hears us—whatever we ask—we know that we have what we asked of him"** (1 John 5:14-15).

Expressing Your Faith Through Prayer

Prayer is one way of expressing your faith to God. If the prayer that follows expresses your sincere desire, consider praying the prayer or putting the thoughts into your own words:

Dear God, I need you. I acknowledge that I have been directing my own life and that, as a result, I have sinned against you. I thank you that you have forgiven my sins through Christ's death on the cross for me. I now invite Christ to take his place on the throne of my life. Take control of my life through the Holy Spirit as you promised you would if I asked in faith. I now thank you for directing my life and for empowering me through the Holy Spirit.

Walking in the Spirit

If you become aware of an area of your life (an attitude or an action) that is displeasing to God, simply confess your sin, and thank God that he has forgiven your sins on the basis of Christ's death on the cross. Accept God's love and forgiveness by faith, and continue to have fellowship with him.

If you find that you've taken back control of your life through sin—a definite act of disobedience—try this exercise, "Spiritual Breathing," as you give that control back to God.

1. Exhale. Confess your sin. Agree with God that you've sinned against him, and thank him for his forgiveness of it, according to 1 John 1:9 and Hebrews 10:1-25. Remember that confession involves repentance, a determination to change attitudes and actions.

2. Inhale. Surrender control of your life to Christ, inviting the Holy Spirit to once again take charge. Trust that he now directs and empowers you, according to the command of Galatians 5:16-17 and the promise of 1 John 5:14-15. Returning to your faith in God enables you to continue to experience God's love and forgiveness.

Revolutionizing Your Marriage

This new commitment of your life to God will enrich your marriage. Sharing with your spouse what you've committed to is a powerful step in solidifying this commitment. As you exhibit the Holy Spirit's work within you, your spouse may be drawn to make the same commitment you've made. If both of you have given control of your lives to the Holy Spirit, you'll be able to help each other remain true to God, and your marriage may be revolutionized. With God in charge of your lives, life becomes an amazing adventure.

Leader's Notes

Contents

About Leading a HomeBuilders Group

What is the leader's job?

Your role is that of "facilitator"—one who encourages people to think and to discover what Scripture says, who helps group members feel comfortable, and who keeps things moving forward.

What is the best setting and time schedule for this study?

This study is designed as a small-group home Bible study. However, it can be adapted for use in a Sunday school setting as well. Here are some suggestions for using this study in a small group and in a Sunday school class:

In a small group

To create a friendly and comfortable atmosphere, it is recommended that you do this study in a home setting. In many cases, the couple that leads the study also serves as host to the group. Sometimes involving another couple as host is a good idea. Choose the option you believe will work best for your group, taking into account factors such as the number of couples participating and the location.

Each session is designed as a ninety-minute study, but we recommend a two-hour block of time. This will allow you to move through each part of the study at a more relaxed pace. However, be sure to keep in mind one of the cardinal rules of a small group: Good groups start *and* end on time. People's time is valuable, and your group will appreciate your being respectful of this.

In a Sunday school class

There are two important adaptations you need to make if you want to use this study in a class setting: (1) The material you cover should focus on the content from the Blueprints section of each session. Blueprints is the heart of each session and is designed to last sixty minutes. (2) Most Sunday school classes are taught in a teacher format instead of a small-group format. If this study will be used in a class setting, the class should adapt to a small-group dynamic. This will involve an interactive, discussion-based format and may also require a class to break into multiple smaller groups (we recommend groups of six to eight people).

What is the best size group?

We recommend from four to eight couples (including you and your spouse). If you have more people interested than you think you can accommodate, consider asking someone else to lead a second group. If you have a large group, you are encouraged at various times in the study to break into smaller subgroups. This helps you cover the material in a timely fashion and allows for optimum interaction and participation within the group.

What about refreshments?

Many groups choose to serve refreshments, which help create an environment of fellowship. If you plan on including refreshments in your study, here are a couple of suggestions: (1) For the first session (or two) you should provide the refreshments and then allow the group to be involved by having people sign up to bring them on later dates. (2) Consider starting your group with a short time of informal fellowship and refreshments (fifteen minutes), then move into the study. If couples are late, they miss only the food and don't disrupt the study. You may also want to have refreshments available at the end of your meeting to encourage fellowship, but remember, respect the group members' time by ending the study on schedule and allowing anyone who needs to leave right away the opportunity to do so gracefully.

What about child care?

Groups handle this differently depending on their needs. Here are a couple of options you may want to consider:

- Have group members be responsible for making their own arrangements.

- As a group, hire child care, and have all the kids watched in one location.

What about prayer?

An important part of a small group is prayer. However, as the leader, you need to be sensitive to the level of comfort the people in your group have toward praying in front of others. Never call on people to pray aloud if you don't know if they are comfortable doing this. There are a number of creative approaches you can take, such as modeling prayer, calling for volunteers, and letting people state their prayers in the form of finishing a sentence. A tool that is helpful in a group is a prayer list. You are encouraged to utilize a prayer list, but let it be someone else's ministry to the group. You should lead the prayer time, but allow another couple in the group the opportunity to create, update, and distribute prayer lists.

In closing

An excellent resource that covers leading a HomeBuilders group in greater detail is the *HomeBuilders Leader Guide* by Drew and Kit Coons. This book may be obtained at your local Christian bookstore or by contacting Group Publishing or FamilyLife.

About the Leader's Notes

The sessions in this study can be easily led without a lot of preparation time. However, accompanying Leader's Notes have been provided to assist you in preparation. The categories within the Leader's Notes are as follows:

Objectives

The purpose of the Objectives is to help focus on the issues that will be presented in each session.

Notes and Tips

This section will relate any general comments about the session. This information should be viewed as ideas, helps, and suggestions. You may want to create a checklist of things you want to be sure to do in each session.

Commentary

Included in this section are notes that relate specifically to Blueprints questions. Not all Blueprints questions in each session will have accompanying commentary notes. Questions with related commentaries are designated by numbers (for example, Blueprints question 3 in Session One would correspond to number 3 in the Commentary section of Session One Leader's Notes).

Session One:
Stressed-Out

Objectives

The first step in learning to overcome stress is gaining a new perspective.

In this session, couples will...

• get to know the other couples in the group.

• identify ways stress affects them individually and in their marriages.

• analyze some common responses to stress.

• look at stress from a biblical perspective.

Notes and Tips

1. For this first session, the focus should be on relaxing and making sure that everyone feels as comfortable as possible. A sense of comfort in the group will allow individuals to more easily share serious issues later on in the study.

As the leader, set a tone of openness by sharing on a personal level. The degree to which you are open and willing to share during this course will have a direct effect on the level of sharing that occurs in the group.

2. If you have not already done so, you will want to read the "About the Sessions" information on pages 4 and 5, as well as "About Leading a HomeBuilders Group" and "About the Leader's Notes" starting on page 102.

3. As part of the first session, you should review with the group some Ground Rules (see p. 10 in the Introduction).

4. Be sure you have a study guide for each person. You will also want to have extra Bibles and pens or pencils.

5. Depending on the size of your group, you may spend longer than fifteen minutes on the Warm-Up section. If this happens, try to finish the Blueprints section in forty-five to sixty minutes. It is a good idea to mark the questions in Blueprints that you want to be sure to cover. Encourage couples to look at any questions you don't get to during the session when they do the HomeBuilders Project for this session.

6. You will notice a note in the margin at the start of the Blueprints section that recommends breaking into smaller groups. The reason for this is twofold: (1) to help facilitate discussion and participation by everyone, and (2) to help you be able to get through the material in the allotted time.

7. With this group just getting under way, it's not too late to invite another couple to join the group. During Wrap-Up, challenge everyone to think about a couple they could invite to the next session.

8. Because this is the first session, make a special point to tell the group about the importance of the HomeBuilders Project before dismissing the couples. Encourage each couple to "Make a

Date" to complete the project before the next meeting. Mention that there will be an opportunity during the next session for couples to report on their experiences with the project.

9. To conclude this first session, you may want to offer a closing prayer instead of asking others to pray aloud. Many people are uncomfortable praying in front of others, and unless you already know your group well, it may be wise to slowly venture into various methods of prayer.

Commentary

Here is some additional information about various Blueprints questions: The numbers that follow correspond to the Blueprints questions of the same numbers in the session. Be aware that notes are not included for every question. Many of the questions in this study are designed for group members to draw from their own opinions and experiences. If you share any of these points, be sure to do so in a manner that does not stifle discussion by making you the authority with *the real answers*. Begin your comments by saying things like, "One thing I notice in this passage is…" or "I think another reason for this is…"

1. In stressful situations the hormone *adrenaline* shoots through the body. The heart beats faster. Arteries constrict. Blood pressure rises. Fats and cholesterol are released into the bloodstream, and blood sugar is increased for energy. Over a prolonged period of time, chemical imbalances develop, and a variety of physical disorders can arise. Prolonged stress can also produce feelings of insecurity, worthlessness, irritability, anger, defensiveness, mental fatigue, diminished concentration, apathy, or sadness.

On the positive side, sometimes stress can be beneficial. For example, in exercise we put stress on our bodies in order to improve our health. The concept of stress not always being negative is addressed later in this session (questions 11 and 12).

3. This question, while potentially identifying some serious issues, should be approached in a spirit of fun. If a group needs help getting their list started, provide a couple of examples of "stress starters." For example, making holiday plans or opening the latest credit card statement, to name a couple.

7. Sometimes stress is magnified when you think your spouse should respond as you do. Understanding your differences will help.

8. Matthew 6:34 relates that problems are a natural part of life (even for Christians—see Matthew 5:45). The challenge becomes not submitting to worry or anxiety.

9. A certain degree of stress is unavoidable. However, when you feel distress, you look upon your problems or situation without optimism or hope.

11. God can work through stressful circumstances to produce perseverance and character in us.

Attention HomeBuilders Leaders

FamilyLife invites you to register your HomeBuilders group. Your registration connects you to the HomeBuilders Leadership Network, a worldwide movement of couples who are using HomeBuilders to strengthen marriages and families in their communities. You'll receive the latest news about HomeBuilders and other ministry opportunities to help strengthen marriages and families in your community. As the HomeBuilders Leadership Network grows, we will offer additional resources such as online training, prayer requests, and chat with authors. There is no cost or obligation to register; simply go to www.familylife.com/homebuilders.

Session Two:
Stress From a Hurried Lifestyle

Objectives

Another key to dealing with stress in marriage is to make wise choices concerning your time and your focus.

In this session, couples will...

• determine where they rank on the hurry scale.

• evaluate a case study of a hurried family.

• recognize the importance of making time with God a priority.

Notes and Tips

1. Because this is the second session, your group members have probably warmed up to one another but may not yet feel free to be completely open about their relationships. Don't force the issue. Continue to encourage couples to attend and to complete the projects.

2. If a couple joins the group for the first time this session, you will want to be sure to introduce them to the other couples. Also, during Warm-Up let them introduce themselves to the group by sharing how and when they met. You should also recap the main points from Session One, and have couples record contact information in their books (p. 16).

3. If you told the group during the first session that you'd be asking them to share something they learned from the first HomeBuilders Project, be sure to ask them. This is an opportunity to establish an environment of accountability. However, be prepared to share a personal example of your own.

4. For Extra Impact: For the reading of the Mary and Martha passage (Luke 10:38-42) in Blueprints (p. 32), have four people from the group volunteer to present the passage. Assign them the roles of Jesus, Mary, Martha, and narrator. Have "Martha" and "Jesus" act out their parts as they read the words of the characters they are playing. "Mary" has no speaking part but should act out her role. The "narrator" can sit off to the side, reading everything except the dialogue. Also, it is helpful if all characters are reading from the same Bible translation.

5. Throughout the sessions in this course, you will find questions that are designed for spouses to answer together (like questions 11 and 12 in this session). The purpose of these questions is to give couples an opportunity to deal with personal issues. While couples are free to share their responses to these questions with the group, respect that not all couples will want to do so.

6. Make sure the arrangements for refreshments (if you're planning to have them) are covered.

7. If your group has decided to use a prayer list, make sure this is covered.

8. For the closing prayer in this session, you may want to ask for a volunteer or two to close the group in prayer. Check ahead of time with a couple of people you think might be comfortable praying aloud.

9. Looking ahead: For the Warm-Up in Session Three, you'll need to round up some cups, rocks, and general household items. Be sure to review and prepare for this exercise prior to the next goup meeting.

Commentary

3. Each statement reflects a common perspective many share, and the net effect in each case is that couples don't have the time together to develop their relationship. In each case Harry and Henrietta should ask themselves whether what they are saying is really true. Is it really true, for example, that they both need to work, or is it that they enjoy a dual income primarily to maintain a more comfortable lifestyle? And will the children truly be deprived if they cut down on their acivities, or do Harry and Henrietta just think they will?

Note: The numbers that follow correspond to the Blueprints questions of the same numbers in the session.

4. If these points don't come up in the group's discussion, you may want to mention these positive, and sometimes overlooked, attributes about Martha: She welcomed Jesus into her home, she was hospitable, she was a hard worker, and she was responsible.

6. Mary recognized that what was most important was spending time with Jesus and listening to his words. Martha seemed more interested in making the right impression with her preparations rather than becoming better acquainted with Jesus.

8. For additional insight into Psalm 46:10a, read this verse from several different Bible versions. It may be that several Bible versions are represented within the group. If not, following are several different Bible versions of Psalm 46:10a:

- *"Be still, and know that I am God"* (King James Version, New King James Version, and New International Version).

- *"Cease striving and know that I am God"* (New American Standard Bible).

- *"Be silent, and know that I am God!"* (New Living Translation).

- *"Step out of the traffic! Take a long, loving look at me, your High God"* (The Message).

- *"Let be and be still, and know (recognize and understand) that I am God"* (The Amplified Bible).

Session Three:
Putting Work in Its Place

Objectives

Reducing stress in marriage requires developing and living with a healthy tension between work and other priorities.

In this session, couples will...

• talk about their jobs and the stress they feel from work.

• examine work from a scriptural perspective.

• evaluate work as related to other priorities.

• consider how to balance the effects that stress from work has on marriage.

Notes and Tips

1. Congratulations! With the completion of this session, you will be halfway through this study. It's time for a checkup: How are you feeling? How is the group going? What has worked well so far? What things might you consider changing as you approach the remaining sessions?

2. For Warm-Up you will need plastic or Styrofoam cups, rocks, and an assortment of small household items.

3. In this session on stress from work, be aware that the terms *work* and *job* are intended to refer to a person's primary job or responsibility. This can refer to what a person does to earn a living, but it also applies to work a person does without pay, such as raising kids.

4. As an example to the group, it is important that you and your spouse complete the HomeBuilders Project each session.

5. Remember the importance of starting and ending on time.

6. During Wrap-Up, make a point to encourage couples to "Make a Date" to complete the HomeBuilders Project for this session.

Commentary

Note: The numbers that follow correspond to the Blueprints questions of the same numbers in the session.

4. A traditional Christian view of priorities is often God first, family second, and then church and/or work as priorities three and four. This hierarchical view of life may not always work very well because we are rarely faced with simple black-and-white choices. For example, let's say you need to decide between meeting with a key client at work or attending your child's soccer game. If the previously mentioned hierarchical view of priorities were in effect, would you always choose your child's soccer game over a meeting with a business client? What if this is your most important client, and the meeting is critical to your company's success? What if you've attended every other soccer game? In reality, the choices we face in life are often complex.

A triathlete balances all three events. As a result, there is always tension, as there is a need to do well in each one. If the athlete succeeds in biking but fails in swimming, the

OVERCOMING STRESS IN YOUR MARRIAGE

race may be lost. In the same way, after the top priority of God, life is lived in tension between family, work, self, community, and church.

5. The priorities in these passages could be summarized as "to love and serve God." The Bible is less clear as to an exact ranking or order for other priorities such as family, work, church, community, and time for self. Life is lived in tension as we try to keep multiple priorities in balance. However, we would be wise to continually practice loving and serving God.

7. Our culture today leads us to believe that success is found through work. We tend to measure our significance by what we do rather than who we are. Indeed, it is not uncommon for people to feel more affirmation at work than at home. This perspective can be dangerous, as work can become an escape or excuse to avoid other responsibilities.

8. For this question, focus on "work" as related to one's paid job.

Session Four:
Money Matters

Objectives

Another key to overcoming stress in marriage is to maintain a proper attitude toward money.

In this session, couples will...

• discuss why finances often cause stress in marriage.

• explore attitudes about money from a biblical perspective.

• reflect on being content with the resources God provides.

• identify ways to invest in their marriages.

Notes and Tips

1. You and your spouse may want to write notes of thanks and encouragement to the couples in your group this week. Thank them for their commitment and contribution to the group, and let them know that you are praying for them. Make a point to pray for them as you write their notes.

2. With the topic of this session revolving around money, you may want to mention to the group that there are a number of good resources available on personal finances from a Christian perspective. Both Ron Blue and Larry Burkett have a number of books on money. There is also a HomeBuilders course, *Mastering Money in Your Marriage*.

3. Work to keep the session on track. In particular, allow enough time for the group to look at some important Scriptures about money that are part of the last question (12) in the Blueprints section.

4. By this time group members should be getting more comfortable with one another. For prayer at the end of this session, you may want to give everyone an opportunity to pray by asking the group to finish a sentence that goes something like this: "Lord, I want to thank you for..." Be sensitive to anyone who may not feel comfortable doing this.

5. You may find it helpful to make some notes right after the meeting to help you evaluate how this session went. Ask yourself questions such as "Did everyone participate?" and "Is there anyone I need to make a special effort to follow up with before the next session?" Asking yourself questions like these will help you stay focused.

6. Looking ahead: For the Warm-Up in Session Five, you'll need a length of string, twine, or yarn for each person in the group.

Commentary

4. Perhaps one of the biggest financial traps we fall into is living beyond our means. This can adversely affect a marriage, regardless of income. Some other problems include wasting money on unneeded items, a preoccupation with buying material things, and differing values about money.

> **Note:** The numbers that follow correspond to the Blueprints questions of the same numbers in the session.

5. In Luke 12:13-15, Jesus warns us that greed comes in multiple forms. One form could be interpreted as materialism: seeking happiness through possessions.

6. People often do not want to think of themselves as greedy, even though greed is difficult to avoid in our culture. Because of this, you might want to help the group think through some of the forms greed takes by asking the following:
- How many TVs did you have in your house as a child compared to now? How many phones?

- How does this comparison help you understand Jesus' warning about greed?

7. Some of the words that might be used to describe the rich man in Luke 12:16-21 include *successful*, *industrious*, *progressive*, *ambitious*, *hardworking*, *diligent*, and *persistent*.

God calls the rich man a fool because the rich man has bought into several false perceptions about money. The man felt content and successful based on his wealth.

10. A common theme in these passages is to trust and be content with God's provision.

Session Five:
Stress From Family Relationships

Objectives

To reduce the marital stress that comes from family relationships, we should practice peacemaking.

In this session, couples will...

- recognize how stress from family relationships can affect a marriage.

- look at the challenge of taking the initiative to resolve conflict and be peacemakers.

- talk about communicating in an effective and understanding way.

Notes and Tips

1. As the leader of a small group, one of the best things you can do for your group is to pray specifically for each group member. Why not take some time to pray as you prepare for this session?

2. With this session's topic revolving around a potentially emotionally charged and sensitive subject (family), keep the tone positive, and be aware of the tendency for discussion on a given question to run long. Be wary not to stifle good discussion, but politely keep things moving forward.

3. For Warm-Up you will need a 6-foot length of string, twine, or yarn for everyone in the group.

4. For Extra Impact: Have a couple present the case study (p. 68) in dramatic fashion as a skit.

5. With the subject of forgiveness being addressed, this is an excellent session to assess where individuals are spiritually. Make a point to follow up with those who are spiritually open but who may have questions. You may want to suggest to the group for further reading the article "Our Problems, God's Answers" in the backs of their books (starting on p. 91).

6. Looking ahead: For the next session—the last session of this study—you may want to have someone, or a couple, share what this study or group has meant to him or her. If this is something you think would be a good idea, think about whom you will ask to share.

Commentary

Note: The numbers that follow correspond to the Blueprints questions of the same numbers in the session.

5. In addition to the obvious problems that arise from broken relationships, the Bible speaks in strong terms about the importance of being willing to forgive (Matthew 6:14-15).

6. Anger can easily lead to depression and bitterness. If you don't go to the person with whom you are angry, the devil—who is the "father of lies" (John 8:44)—can lead you to believe all kinds of falsehoods about a person and situation.

8. We should take the initiative in resolving conflict, especially when we have offended someone.

9. Forgiveness, the willingness to forgive others as well as a willingness to seek forgiveness, should be an ongoing part of the Christian life. God modeled this for us, taking the initiative to reconcile us to himself through the sacrifice of his Son, Jesus.

11. Suggest these responses if the group doesn't come up with something similar: Rod should have sought to understand Cindy instead of trying to solve her problems. Rod should have recognized Cindy's need for understanding and placed that above his needs. Rod should have identified some of the feelings Cindy was experiencing and given her the freedom to talk about them without judging her or offering advice. A good first step would have been for Rob to ask, "How can I help you?" or "What do you need from me?"

Session Six
Stress From Hardships

Objectives

Stress from the hardships of life can drive a couple apart unless they recognize the trials as an opportunity to draw closer to God.

In this session, couples will...

• analyze the effects hardships have had on their marriages.

• study hardships from a biblical perspective.

• affirm their need to believe God.

Notes and Tips

1. If you believe someone in your group has questions about what a Christian is, this final session might be a good opportunity to take a few minutes to explain how you became a Christian and the difference Christ has made in your life.

2. While this study from the HomeBuilders Couples Series has great value, people are likely to return to previous patterns of living unless they commit to a plan for carrying on the progress made through the study. During this final session of the course, encourage couples to take specific steps beyond this study to keep their marriages growing. For example, you may want to challenge couples who have developed the habit of a "date night" during the course of this study to continue this practice. Also, you may want the group to consider doing another study from this series.

3. If you discover in this session that some couples are in exceptionally difficult situations, privately encourage them to seek help from a professional counselor.

4. As a part of this, the last session, you may want to consider devoting some time to plan for one more meeting—a party to celebrate the completion of this study!

Commentary

2. Hardships often reveal and amplify already existing weaknesses in a marriage. For example, if a couple has a communication problem, and then a hardship comes, they don't know how to talk to each other about the pain they are experiencing. This can lead to feelings of discouragement and hopelessness.

Note: The numbers that follow correspond to the Blueprints questions of the same numbers in the session.

4. Notice that this passage does not state that the trials we face in life are a joy but that we are to consider them as if they were a joy. In the face of difficult circumstances, our outlook or mental attitude is important. Even if we don't feel joy during a trial, we can choose to respond, in faith, as if we do.

6. To help better understand exactly what James means when he advises us to ask God for wisdom, here is a description of wisdom: Wisdom is the ability to take knowledge and apply it in practical ways. Wisdom is not some kind of ethereal knowledge or insight, but it is skill for living. It's taking the raw components of life and making something meaningful out of them.

In the middle of a trial, we need wisdom to know how to live and endure in a trying situation. God gives us wisdom not to escape from a trial but to grow through it.

8. During hardships it's not uncommon for people, Christians included, to question God, asking, "Why did you allow this to happen?" or "How could a loving God allow this?"

9. As stated in James 1:6, if we ask God for wisdom in doubt, we are "like a wave of the sea, blown and tossed by the wind." When we doubt God over the wisdom he gives, we feel unsettled because we are not drawing upon his comfort and strength.

Does Your Church Offer Marriage Insurance?

Great marriages don't just happen—husbands and wives need to nurture them. They need to make their marriage relationship a priority.

That's where the HomeBuilders Couples Series® can help! The series consists of interactive 6- to 7-week small group studies that make it easy for couples to really open up with each other. The result is fun, non-threatening interactions that build stronger Christ-centered relationships between spouses—and with other couples!

Whether you've been married for years or are newly married, this series will help you and your spouse discover timeless principles from God's Word that you can apply to your marriage and make it the best it can be!

The HomeBuilders Leader Guide gives you all the information and encouragement you need to start and lead a dynamic HomeBuilders small group.

The HomeBuilders Couples Series includes these life-changing studies:
- Building Teamwork in Your Marriage
- Building Your Marriage *(also available in Spanish!)*
- Building Your Mate's Self-Esteem
- Growing Together in Christ
- Improving Communication in Your Marriage *(also available in Spanish!)*
- Making Your Remarriage Last
- Mastering Money in Your Marriage
- Overcoming Stress in Your Marriage
- Resolving Conflict in Your Marriage

And check out the HomeBuilders Parenting Series!
- Building Character in Your Children
- Establishing Effective Discipline for Your Children
- Guiding Your Teenagers
- Helping Your Children Know God
- Improving Your Parenting
- Raising Children of Faith

Look for the **HomeBuilders Couples Series and HomeBuilders Parenting Series** at your favorite Christian supplier or write: